Draw or paste a picture of yourself here.

THIS IS ME.

AND THIS IS MY BOOK.

EVERYBODY ELSE KEEP OUT!

Goodbye, House

by Ann Banks and Nancy Evans

Illustrations by Marisabina Russo

H

Harmony Books
New York

For our parents

Acknowledgments

We would like to thank the children who gave us their advice about what makes a good move and the parents who shared their experiences about moving with children. Special thanks go to Isabel Banks, Charlotte Evans, the Mill Hill School (Southport, Connecticut) fourth grade, Shelley Richtmyer and friends, Suzanne Lainson, Louise Bernikow, Marcy Posner, and of course Delia Ephron, Lorrie Bodger, and Seymour Wishman. For their enthusiastic support, our gratitude goes to our editor, Harriet Bell; our illustrator, Marisabina Russo; and Ken Sansone.

Designed by Jane Borkow

ISBN 0-517-53907-1

20 19 18 17 16 15 14 13 12 11

Goodbye, House

My name: _____

My address: _____

_____

My age: _____

My grade: _____

My height: _____

My weight: _____

Today's date: _____

I am moving from _____

to _____ .

My new address: _____

_____

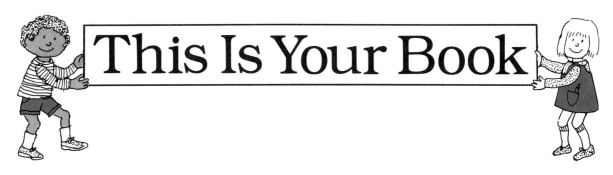

This Is Your Book

Your parents tell you you're going to move. Maybe you hate the idea, maybe you're looking forward to it. However you feel, the next few months can be a confusing time. Your parents will be busy making plans for the move and for your new home. You may feel left out. *Goodbye, House* is a place where you can make your own plans for the move. There will be many things on your mind. You may wonder why you have to go at all. After all, this move wasn't *your* idea. You'll be sad to leave your friends, and you won't want to forget them. You may be wondering what your new school will be like and how soon you'll be able to make new friends.

There are projects in *Goodbye, House* to begin right now, and projects to do as you get ready for the move, and projects to complete while you're getting settled in your new home.

Before you move, you'll

★ draw a picture of your old house.

★ paste in your friends' pictures and write down their addresses.

★ give postcards to your friends so they'll be sure to write you.

★ make a list of people you'll want to say goodbye to.

★ learn about the town you're moving to.

★ look at a map to see where you're moving and how far it is.

★ make a list of what you want to take with you.

★ plan how to fix up your new room.

★ make a list of ways you can help your parents during the move.

And...

After you move, you'll

★ draw a map of your new neighborhood so you won't get lost.

★ find a secret hiding place in your new home.

★ plan your first day of school.

★ make a list of what you want to show and tell your new classmates.

When you have completed all the projects, *Goodbye, House* will be a scrapbook of your favorite memories from your old home and your first feelings about your new home.

 # My Family

My father's name is _____ .

His birthday is _____ .

My father's job is _____ .

My father likes to _____ .

My mother's name is _____ .

Her birthday is _____ .

My mother's job is _____ .

My mother likes to _____ .

I have _____ brothers and _____ sisters.

Their names are _____ .

Their birthdays are _____ .

Their favorite sports and hobbies are _____

_____ .

Getting Ready to Move

Draw or paste in a picture of your old house.

Address: _____

_____

My Favorite Memories

There are things you'll want to remember after you've moved. The time you hit a home run. The play you put on with your friends. The vacation picnic at the lake. The time you went to an amusement park. Your first horse ride. Your secret clubhouse. A special tree.

So you don't forget, write your favorite memories here.

I remember

I remember

I remember

I remember

Take a leaf from your yard or a park and paste it here.

The person I will miss most is _____ .

What I like to do most in the winter is _____

_____

_____ .

My favorite places to visit are _____

_____

_____ .

The thing I like best about my old house is _____

_____

_____ .

My favorite place to play is _____ .

What I like to do most in the summer is _____

_____

_____ .

My other favorite memories are _____

_____

_____ .

My Favorite Places and People

On these two pages, draw or paste pictures of some of your favorite places and people.

How I Feel About Moving

Your feelings may change as moving day gets closer. They will probably change again after you first move into your new home, and again after you've been in your new town for a few weeks. So in the coming weeks, return to this page whenever you feel like writing down your feelings. Put the date next to each entry you make.

Secret Treasure

So your old home doesn't forget you, bury something in your yard or a favorite place. Make it something that is special to you. . . . Your lucky stone. A marble. A pinecone. A picture you've drawn. Seashells. A toy whistle. A snakeskin. Look through your junk drawer for other ideas. Put a piece of paper with your name, age, and the date on it, and a secret message if you wish, in a jar with a tight lid. Bury that with your treasure.

On this page, draw a map of where your treasure is buried. You may want to come back and dig it up someday.

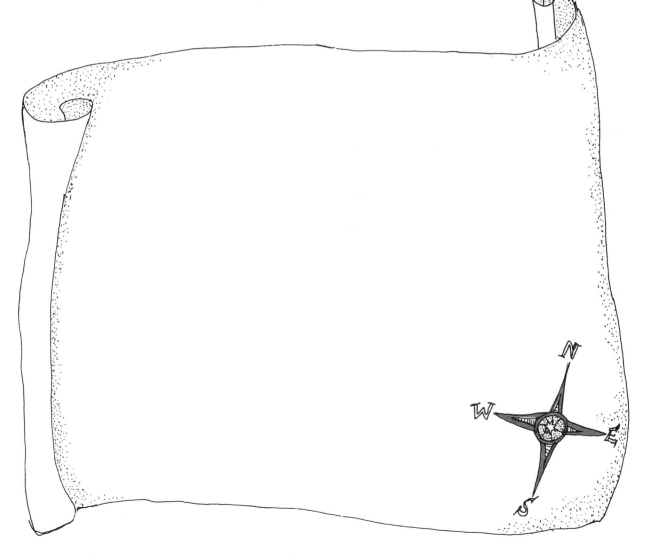

My Special Friends

Ask your favorite friends for their pictures to paste here. Fill in each friend's name and birthday and favorite things next to the picture.

Name: _____

Birthday: _____

My friend's favorite things:

• Television show _____

• Singer _____

• Movie star _____

• Book _____

• Hobby _____

• Sport _____

• School subject _____

• Animal _____

Name: _____

Birthday: _____

My friend's favorite things:

• Television show _____

• Singer _____

• Movie star _____

• Book _____

• Hobby _____

• Sport _____

• School subject _____

• Animal _____

Name: _____

Birthday: _____

My friend's favorite things:

- Television show _____
- Singer _____
- Movie star _____
- Book _____
- Hobby _____
- Sport _____
- School subject _____
- Animal _____

Name: _____

Birthday: _____

My friend's favorite things:

- Television show _____
- Singer _____
- Movie star _____
- Book _____
- Hobby _____
- Sport _____
- School subject _____
- Animal _____

My New Pen Pals

Just because you're moving away doesn't mean you'll forget your friends. So many new things will be happening, you'll have plenty to write them about. You can send postcards during your trip. Or send a picture of your new home when you arrive. Describe the things that will be new and exciting to your friends. Will you be seeing snow for the first time? Is there a special playground near your new home?

Fill in this list with the names, addresses, and phone numbers of your friends so you can write or call them.

Name _____

Address _____

_____ **Telephone Number** _____

Name _____

Address _____

_____ **Telephone Number** _____

Name _____

Address _____

_____ **Telephone Number** _____

Name _____

Address _____

_____ **Telephone Number** _____

Name _____

Address _____

_____ **Telephone Number** _____

Name _____

Address _____

_____ **Telephone Number** _____

Name _____

Address _____

_____ **Telephone Number** _____

Name _____

Address _____

_____ **Telephone Number** _____

Name _____

Address _____

_____ **Telephone Number** _____

Name _____

Address _____

_____ **Telephone Number** _____

Name _____

Address _____

_____ **Telephone Number** _____

Ask your mother or father to get you prestamped postcards, and then write your name and your new address on them. Give them to your closest friends so they can write to you at your new home.

Goodbye, Friends

Who are the people that you want to be sure to say goodbye to? You don't want to forget anybody important. Write in the names of the people you might like to see before you leave. Put a check mark beside each name when you say goodbye.

▶ My best friends

Goodbye _____

Goodbye _____

Goodbye _____

Goodbye _____

▶ My teacher

Goodbye _____

▶ My scout troop leader

Goodbye _____

▶ My music teacher

Goodbye _____

▶ My baseball coach

Goodbye _____

▶ My favorite neighbors

Goodbye _____

Goodbye _____

Goodbye _____

▶ My baby-sitter

Goodbye _____

Now make your list of other special people to say goodbye to.

▶ Goodbye _____

▶ Goodbye _____

▶ Goodbye _____

▶ Goodbye _____

▶ Goodbye _____

▶ Goodbye _____

▶ Goodbye _____

▶ Goodbye _____

▶ Goodbye _____

▶ Goodbye _____

See if you can have a goodbye party with your friends. Ask all your friends to bring you something to remember them by—a snapshot of themselves, their favorite joke written on a piece of paper, a baseball card.

# Goodbye, Old School

Name of my school: _____

How I get to school: _____

My teacher's name: _____

My principal's name: _____

Number of kids in my class: _____

Number of girls: _____

Number of boys: _____

School colors: _____

Name of school team: _____

Most popular sport at my school: _____

Favorite after-school activity at my school: _____

Draw a picture of your old school.

My New Home

If you're moving far away, before you move learn as much as you can about the place you're moving to. You'll want to know how big your new state is, and where it is, and what the weather is like. You'll want to learn about your new town, too. You can find the answers with an encyclopedia and an almanac or a map. Ask your parents, the librarian, or your teacher to help you.

The name of my new town is _____ .

The population of my new town is _____ .

My new town is in the state of _____ .

My new state is bordered by the states of _____

_____ .

The capital of my new state is _____ .

My state's sports teams are _____

_____ .

The climate in my new state is _____ Hot _____ Cold

_____ Rainy _____ Dry _____ Windy

If you're moving only a short distance, will you go to the same school?

_____

Use the same public library? _____

My new home is at _____ .
                                                  (address)
The number of rooms in my new home is _____ .

The color of my new home is _____ .

Write to the Chamber of Commerce for information about your new town. Do this early so you'll be sure to receive the material before you move. Send a postcard to: Chamber of Commerce, Your New Town, Your New State. Ask your parents for the zip code number.

There may be children living in the house or apartment you'll be moving to. If there are, write or call and ask them to make a list for you of fun things to do, places to visit, and children in the neighborhood.

Ask your mother or father to help you write a letter to your new school to see if you can get a pen pal from your new class before you arrive. You can exchange pictures, and ask how big the school is and what games the kids play.

Find out who is moving into the house you're leaving. If the family has children about your age, make a list of the things that are fun to do in your neighborhood and the friends they might like to meet. Wish them a nice stay in your old home.

Good Riddance

Thank goodness! Finally you'll be rid of all those things you hate. What will you be glad to leave behind? A fierce dog? A nickname you hate? Silly rules at school? The bully on the block? The mess in your room?

- Good riddance _____

- Good riddance _____

- Good riddance _____

- Good riddance _____

- Good riddance _____

I Can't Wait!

What are you looking forward to about where you'll live after your move? Maybe you'll get to ride a bus to school. Maybe you'll be near a park with a wonderful playground. Maybe you'll be near a beach. Maybe you'll finally have a room of your own. Maybe there's a good climbing tree nearby. Maybe you'll live in an apartment building with an elevator.

Ask your mom or dad what new things you'll get to do and see at your new town. Write them down here.

I can't wait to _____

_____.

I can't wait to _____

_____.

I can't wait to _____

_____.

I can't wait to _____

_____.

Worries

Any move will bring a lot of changes for you and your family. Some you'll be looking forward to. Others may be scary. It's a help to remember that you aren't the only one who's ever had to move. Millions of children move every year. Here are some of the things that other kids have worried about. If you have any of these worries, you'll feel better if you talk them over with your parents or a friend before the move.

- What if nobody talks to you the first day of school?

- What if your teacher doesn't like you?

- What if the neighborhood kids won't let you join their club?

- What if no kids live on your new block?

- What if you're behind in school?

- What if your birthday comes soon after the move? Will you have any new friends to help you celebrate?

- What if you don't get invited to any parties?

- What if you're moving farther away from your grandparents? When will you see them again?

- What if your new school's so big you get lost?

- What if your clothes are different from what all the other kids wear?

- What if you're moving to a smaller home? Will you still be able to have friends stay over?

A New Start

Imagine that you've already moved. What do you want your new life to be like? Are there things about yourself you'd like to change? Ways that you'd like things to be different?

I will try to _____

_____

_____

_____

_____

_____

I will try not to _____

_____

_____

_____

_____

_____

My New Room

Ask your parents what your new room will look like. Ask them:

How many windows will there be? _____

Will you be sharing your room? _____

Whom will you be sharing it with? _____

Will you have bunk beds? _____

What color are the walls in your new room? _____

If you could paint your new room any color, what would it be? _____

You'll feel better if you can fix up your room right away. So start thinking now about where you will put your favorite things.

What will you put on the walls? A poster of your favorite TV star? A baseball pennant? Your swimming certificate? Make a list.

_____

_____

_____

_____

_____

_____

Will you have a desk? _____

Will you have a bookcase? _____

Will you be getting anything new especially for your new room? _____

What will it be? _____

My Pets

Do you have a pet? _____

What kind of pet do you have? _____

What is your pet's name? _____

What does your pet eat? _____

How often do you feed your pet? _____

Does your pet have a favorite toy? _____

What is it? _____

How will your pet travel to your new home? _____ Plane _____ Car _____ Train

Will you be taking care of your pet on the trip? _____

What will you need to bring? Special food? Water dish? Leash?

_____

After you move, your pet will probably be able to tell that things are different. Give him special attention when you get to your new home so he doesn't get upset. Pet him a lot or take him for walks.

If you have to leave your pet behind

What will happen to your pet? Some pets, like lizards or hamsters, are really hard to move. Or maybe your dog wouldn't be happy if you're moving to an apartment. If you think about this ahead of time, you can make sure your pet will have a good new home. Give the new owners a postcard with your new address on it. Ask them to write and tell you how your pet is doing.

31

Helping Out

You can help get ready to move by

- ▶ returning books to the library.

- ▶ cleaning out your school locker.

- ▶ deciding which toys you don't want anymore, and giving them away.

- ▶ running errands for your parents.

- ▶ helping with brothers and sisters.

Other ways to help are:

1. _____

2. _____

3. _____

4. _____

5. _____

Remember that your parents are leaving their home and friends, too. Surprise them by doing nice things. If you bring your mother a glass of lemonade while she's packing, you will both feel better.

If you're going to be around the day the movers come, find out ahead of time what you can do to help. Maybe you want to offer to run last-minute errands for your parents. Maybe you'd rather spend the day saying goodbye to your friends.

Before you move, you might want to give some of your old toys or books to the Salvation Army or to the children's hospital. Sit down with your parents and decide what you want to give away and whom it should go to.

Or ask if you can have a yard sale to sell the things you don't want to take to your new house or apartment.

So that your magazines arrive at your new home, change the address for your magazine subscriptions several weeks before you move.

Planning My Trip

Ask your mom or dad about plans for the trip. Find out how you're going to get to your new home. Maybe you will fly with your mom while your dad drives. Maybe you will stay at your grandmother's or be at camp while the moving is done.

If your family drives, there will be things to look forward to about the trip. You might stay at a motel with a swimming pool or stop at a special landmark. Ask your parents to show you on a map where you will be going, and what cities and states you will fly over or drive through to get there.

If you are moving inside the same city, mark both places on a city map, and draw on the map the way to get to your new home.

After you've talked to your parents about the trip, write down the answers here.

What day will the moving van come? _____

What day will you leave? _____

How will you travel? _____
(car, bus, train, plane)

How many miles will you travel? _____

How long will it take? _____

How many states will you go through? _____

Will you stay in a motel? _____

How many nights? _____

Who will be making the trip with you? _____

_____

_____

Just before you move, send a welcoming postcard to yourself at your new home.

My Own Suitcase

What do you want to take? Pretend you are already on your way, and think of what you'd like with you on the trip. Think of what you'll want for the first night in your new house, too.

- Books
- Stuffed animal
- Diary
- Baseball glove
- Favorite pajamas
- Special pillow
- Night-light

- _____
- _____
- _____
- _____
- _____
- _____
- _____

My Trip to My New House

Draw or paste in a picture of your family on moving day.

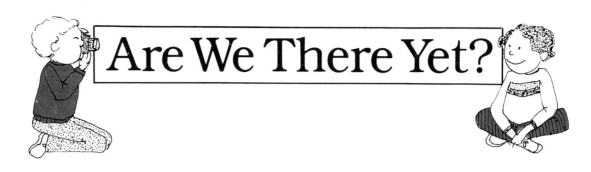

Are We There Yet?

Be sure and take *Goodbye, House* with you on moving day so you can keep a record of the trip.

★My Trip Record★

Date of the trip: _____

We are traveling from _____ to _____

_____.

The trip will take _____ hours/days.

We left at _____ o'clock.

We are traveling by _____.

The trip is about _____ miles.

We played these games: _____

_____

We sang these songs: _____

_____

Here are the places we saw: _____

_____

_____

We spent the night at _____.

We arrived at _____ o'clock on _____.

When you get to your new home, use your trip record to write postcards to your old friends telling them about your trip and your arrival.

Paste in souvenirs from your trip.

My New Home

Draw or paste in a picture of your new house.

Address: _____

_____

We're Here!

Hello, House! Now that you've arrived at your new home, you'll want to learn your way around as soon as you can.

★ The first thing to do is find your room.

★ Make a sign with your name on it to put on the door.

★ Bring your suitcase to your room.

★ Look out your windows. What do you see? _____

_____

★ Look up and down the street. See if there are any bicycles or kickballs.

★ Ask your parents what you can do to help.

★ You might want to save a box from the movers to make a playhouse.

★ Ask for a flashlight so you can find your way around in the dark.

Finding My Way Around

This list of your important places and how to get there can be filled in as you learn your way around your new neighborhood. Until you memorize your new address and phone number, print them on a small piece of paper and carry it with you. Also, you may want to include the phone numbers where your parents work. Extra spaces on your new neighborhood chart are for adding more of your favorite places.

	Name	How I will get there (walk, bus, bicycle, car)
School		
Public library		
Movie theater		
Toy store		
Playground		

My New Neighborhood

Draw a picture or a map of your new neighborhood, showing where you live and all the places you like to go. If you want to, cut out pictures from magazines that remind you of your favorite places: a book could mean the library, and a ballet shoe your dancing class. Then paste them on the map.

Find a secret hiding place in your new home. Do *not* put your secret hiding place on this map.

The Night Before My First Day of School

What time will you leave for school? _____ o'clock

Will you be going to the same school
as any of your brothers and sisters? _____ yes _____ no

How will you get there? _____ Bus _____ Walk _____ Car

Will anyone be coming with you? _____ yes _____ no

Who? _____ Parent _____ Neighbor _____ Older brother or sister

What will you wear? List the clothes you'll be wearing and put them out for tomorrow morning.

_____

_____

_____

_____

Will you bring your own lunch? _____ yes _____ no

What other things will you take with you? Put a check mark next to each thing you'll need for school. Then put the things together in one pile.

_____ Pencil box   _____ Notebook   _____ Bus pass

_____ Eraser   _____ Ruler   _____ Lunch money

_____ Pencils   _____ Book bag

46

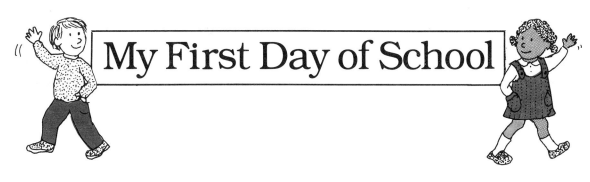

My First Day of School

What is your teacher's name? _____

What does your teacher look like? _____

Were you assigned a locker? _____ yes _____ no

What did you do in class? (Draw pictures? Read stories?)

_____

_____

What did you have for lunch? _____

How many recesses were there? _____

What did you do at recess? _____

Whom did you meet? _____

Did you have an assembly? _____ yes _____ no

Write down how you felt about the first day of school.

 # Hello, New School

Name of school: _____

How I get to school: _____

My teacher's name: _____

My principal's name: _____

Number of kids in my class: _____

Number of girls: _____

Number of boys: _____

School colors: _____

Name of school team: _____

Number of recesses: _____

Most popular sport at my new school: _____

Favorite after-school activity at my new school: _____

Draw a picture of your new school.

Draw a picture of your teacher.

School Diary:
The First Weeks

There will probably be things about your new school that you like, and some things you can't stand. You may be ahead in some subjects and behind in others. There will be new school rules to remember. Your new friends may wear different clothes and play different games.

At first, everything may seem so different that you feel scared. But after a while, you'll begin to feel more at home. On these next pages, you can write down what you see, hear, and feel during your first weeks at school.

Your classroom:

Are the desks arranged in a circle or in rows? _____

Who sits next to you? _____

Do you sit in the front of the room or in the back? _____

How many windows are there? _____

What does your new classroom have that your old one didn't?

_____

_____

Your school:

Does your school playground have these?

       Swings   _____ yes _____ no

       Jungle gym   _____ yes _____ no

       Baseball diamond _____ yes _____ no

       Basketball hoop   _____ yes _____ no

Check which games you play:

       Jump rope

       Hopscotch

       Kickball

       Basketball

       Baseball

       Others _____

                 _____

                 _____

Is there an auditorium?   _____ yes _____ no

Is there a school library?   _____ yes _____ no

Can you talk in the halls?   _____ yes _____ no

Do you stand in line for your bus? _____ yes _____ no

What do you like best about your new school? _____

_____

_____

_____

_____

What do you like least about your new school? _____

_____

_____

_____

Schoolwork:

Is there more homework than in your old school? _____ yes _____ no

How long does it take you to do it? _____

Is your new teacher harder than your old teacher? _____ yes _____ no

Are there subjects you're ahead in? _____ yes _____ no

     What are they? _____

Are there subjects you're behind in? _____ yes _____ no

     What are they? _____

What is your favorite subject? _____

What is your least favorite subject? _____

Do you have any subjects in your new school
that you didn't have in your old school? _____ yes _____ no

     What are they? _____

Do you have a gym teacher? _____ yes _____ no

     What is your gym teacher's name? _____

Do you have an art teacher? _____ yes _____ no

     What is your art teacher's name? _____

Do you have a music teacher? _____ yes _____ no

     What is your music teacher's name? _____

Are there clubs in your school that
do interesting things?   _____ yes _____ no

     What are they? _____

     Which ones will you join? _____

Classmates:

How do kids dress at your new school? _____

_____

_____

How is the way they dress different from the way your old friends dressed?

_____

_____

How do you feel different from the kids in the class? _____

_____

_____

_____

Are there class officers? _____ yes _____ no

     Who are they? _____

     _____

My New Friends

Who are your friends? List your new friends in the order of your favorites.

1. _____

2. _____

3. _____

4. _____

5. _____

Find out about your new friends. Fill in the answers below.

My friend is _____ .

The color of my friend's hair is _____ .

The color of my friend's eyes is _____ .

My friend's birthday is _____ .

My friend's middle name is _____ .

My friend has _____ brothers and sisters.

My friend is _____ .

The color of my friend's hair is _____ .

The color of my friend's eyes is _____ .

My friend's birthday is _____ .

My friend's middle name is _____ .

My friend has _____ brothers and sisters.

My friend is _____ .

The color of my friend's hair is _____ .

The color of my friend's eyes is _____ .

My friend's birthday is _____ .

My friend's middle name is _____ .

My friend has _____ brothers and sisters.

My friend is _____ .

The color of my friend's hair is _____ .

The color of my friend's eyes is _____ .

My friend's birthday is _____ .

My friend's middle name is _____ .

My friend has _____ brothers and sisters.

My friend is _____ .

The color of my friend's hair is _____ .

The color of my friend's eyes is _____ .

My friend's birthday is _____ .

My friend's middle name is _____ .

My friend has _____ brothers and sisters.

Hello, Friends

Your new classmates will want to know about you, too. They'll want to know about your family, where you live, and what you think about your new town and school. They'll want to know what you like to do and what you're good at. Underline the activities you can do. Put two lines under those you're really good at. Can you do any of these?

Play a sport

What sport do you play? _____

Play a musical instrument

What instrument do you play? _____

What is your favorite song to play? _____

Make candy or cookies

Do card tricks

Sing

Do cartwheels

Draw cartoons

Whistle

Stand on your head

Do puppet shows

Other things I can do are:

_____

_____

_____

_____

_____

Me and My Friends

Draw or paste pictures of yourself and your friends at school, at the playground, or at home.

What I Don't Like About My New Home

I don't like...

What I Like About My New Home

I like...

My New Home:
The First-Year Anniversary

Wait until you've been in your new home a year to fill in this page. Read over everything you wrote in *Goodbye, House* about how you felt when you first learned you were going to move and just after you moved. Are you feeling differently now? What do you still miss about your old home? What do you like better about where you live now? What surprises have there been for you?

Goodbye, House: A Parents' Guide

Each year 15 million families move. That means 34.5 million children under the age of twelve leave their friends to face the trauma of being the new kid on the block. Although many children's books have been written on the subject of moving, there is no book that allows the child to create his own version of the transition. *Goodbye, House,* an activities book for the school-age child, invites your child to express and order his feelings as he chronicles the family move in his very own book. And, important to child and parent alike, it gives him something to *do* during a period of possible loneliness and disorientation.

Goodbye, House engages the child in projects from the moment she is first told about the impending move until she feels truly comfortable in her new town. As she fills in the spaces in the book, the child will gain a sense of mastery over the new environment and the feeling of overwhelming newness will diminish. Once the adjustment is made and the book completed, *Goodbye, House* will serve as a scrapbook that can be looked at fondly.

The most important function of *Goodbye, House* is as a diary in which the child can feel free to express all her feelings, the good and the bad, about the move. By writing down what she feels when she first hears about the move and again as moving day approaches and later when she arrives in the new town, she will be able to acknowledge and clarify the range of emotions she will be passing through. She will also be better able to discuss her feelings with you.

Because this is the child's personal book, each child from six to twelve years old in your family should have his or her own copy. We suggest you take the time now to read *Goodbye, House* before your child begins to fill it in. By reading the text now, you'll know what questions your child will be likely to ask in the weeks ahead.

In the following pages our intention is not to offer advice on how to find a mover, pack your belongings, and contact Welcome Wagon. There are a number of good moving guides available. Instead, what we offer are general suggestions to help you make the move easier for your child, and specific suggestions to help your child use *Goodbye, House* to best advantage. They are suggestions, not hard and fast rules. Our hope is that the shared wisdom

and experiences of other parents and children will encourage you to choose and create your own strategies for making your move the happiest possible.

• **Tell your child as soon as possible about the move.** You might think it would be best to hold off until the last moment. But children can usually sense when something's going on. So think of the early announcement as giving your child time to adjust rather than time to worry. What you don't want is for your child to hear about the move inadvertently from neighbors or friends before he hears it from you.

• **Be honest about the reasons for the move.** When the move is a matter of choice—for instance, whether to take a new job or promotion—many parents like to bring their children into the discussion to ask them how they feel about it. After all, the kids' lives are going to be affected by the choice that is made.

If the move is necessitated by a divorce, by loss of a job, by financial problems, by a death in the family, the children should understand what's going on. Keeping them in the dark or smoothing over the details will only further aggravate their anxiety. The more frank you are with your children, the more they will be encouraged to be honest with you about their feelings.

• **Don't hide your own doubts about the move.** By all means point out the advantages of where you'll be moving, but don't forget to give your children the idea that it's normal to be sad about leaving their old life behind. Let them know that you, too, have some regrets about moving. On the other hand, don't assume that all your fears are shared by your children. Some kids adjust to moving more easily than their parents imagine.

• **Consider the timing of the move.** Common wisdom used to say that the best time to move was during the summer so children could start school with the rest of the class in September. Now there is a debate about whether it's better to move your children during the school year or during the summer. There are compelling reasons on both sides.

Those who advocate moving during the school

year say that a child gets more attention from students and teachers than he would if he started school in the fall along with everybody else. After all, they say, the first day of school is a big day for all students, and the teacher isn't likely to give your child much special attention because as far as she's concerned, every child is "new."

The kids we talked to had differing opinions about the best time of year to move. One child, for example, told us she thought it was scary coming in during the school year because "everyone is already friends." On the other hand, another child who's moved eight times says he finds the summer hardest because so many kids are away on family vacations and at camp. His first choice is to move at the end of the summer right before school starts. No matter when you move, there are advantages to be pointed out to your kids.

• **Inform your children's teachers about the move as soon as you tell the children.** If your child's classroom behavior changes, the teacher will take into account that the move is on her mind.

• **Spend extra time with your child.** Just when there are heavy practical demands on your time, your child will need you more than ever. It's worth taking time out from your busy schedule to pay special attention to your child so problems don't arise later.

• **Connect your child's growing up with the move.** Your move may coincide with a new developmental stage in your child's maturity. If so, you can encourage him to connect the move in a positive way with how grown up he is becoming. For example, if he is now old enough to ride the bus by himself, you could offer him the chance to take the bus to visit his old neighborhood.

• **Allow your child to fantasize.** For many children, the idea of moving evokes powerful fantasies of a fresh start: they'll leave behind a nickname they despise, they'll always keep their rooms neat after the move. Even if they are unable to realize those fantasies, don't tease them about it.

• **Read children's stories about moving.** One way for your child to work out her fears about moving is to give her storybooks about other kids who have moved and survived. You can ask the children's librarian or your moving company to suggest titles.

• **Help ease your child's fears about leaving old friends.** Children worry that when they move all their old friends will forget them. Many of the projects in *Goodbye, House* are designed to give children the sense that the move doesn't mean that their past life is irretrievably lost. Here are ways you can help.

1. Suggest to your child that she can keep in touch with her old friends. If you're moving a short distance, let her know that her old friends can come visit and she can return to her old neighborhood.

For long-distance moves, you may want to promise that she can call her best friends long distance on their birthdays.

For short- and long-distance moves, we've suggested your child hand out to friends pre-stamped postcards (available at your post office) with her name and new address. That way she can be sure to get some mail her first weeks at her new home.

Although most children won't need encouragement, writing old friends about a new home may help them look on the bright side and give them a chance to express their feelings. Your child may want to include a picture of her new home or room in the letter.

2. Encourage him to say goodbye to special people. Children who are normally outgoing may have an attack of shyness when they are moving. They may need encouragement, but they will feel better if they make the effort to say goodbye to people like their school bus driver or music teacher. You might also want to let your child pick out a small gift for people who have been especially nice to him, such as a favorite baby-sitter or neighbor.

3. Plan a going-away party. Some teachers are amenable to having a party in the classroom at the end of the school day if the parents supply the snacks and drinks. Or you may choose to have a party at home. Some families like to have a farewell open house for both kids and adults before the move. Take pictures of your child and her friends at the party. Later she may want to paste them into *Goodbye, House.* Consider giving your child an autograph book so she can pass it out to her friends at the party.

4. Lend your child a camera. For some of the projects in *Goodbye, House* we've asked your child to paste in a photograph. A picture of where you live now, for instance, should be a comforting reminder in the first few weeks at the new home. If your child is old enough, lend or give him an inexpensive camera. Otherwise, you may have photographs on hand he could paste into *Goodbye, House.*

• **Help your child make his change of address.** *Goodbye, House* includes an address and phone number listing for old friends, which the child can fill out himself by asking his friends or using a phone book. When it's completed before the move, he will have a permanent record of how to get in touch with his special friends.

Get enough change-of-address postcards from the post office to give some to your child. He can use them to change magazine subscriptions and to pass out to friends.

• **Help your child learn about her new home.** This is an occasion for your child to use skills learned in making class reports to help her in her own life. *Goodbye, House* has projects for children to learn about where they're moving to: climate, population, neighboring states. The information can be found in children's reference books, but your child may ask you for help. Giving your child her own map of the area you'll be moving to would be helpful. We also have suggested that your child write to the Chamber of Commerce for information about where you're moving, and your child may want help with that project as well.

• **Prepare your child for whether his pets will move or not.** If you're moving to a place where pets are not allowed or if they can't come with you for some other reason, explain the situation to your child and discuss what he thinks would be best to do. Is there a friend or a nice couple down the block who might like the pet? Once a new owner is found, allow the child to be present when the transfer is made. If possible, let him see where his pet will be staying. Your child may want to write instructions for the new owner explaining how to take care of his pet. He can also give the new owner a postcard to write news of his pet's well-being.

If the pet will be making the move with you, decide with your child how the pet will be cared for during the move. On moving day, your child may want to be responsible for keeping his dog or cat out of the movers' way. Enough people have told of a pet panicking and running off on moving day that it seems clear that pets sense the impending move and need as much special attention as anyone else.

• **Make lists with your child** of ways she can help out before the trip, on the day of the move, and when you arrive.

• **Allow your child to participate in cleaning out and packing.** One woman, now a mother of two, recalls the weeding out she had to do as a child for her family's numerous moves: "Every time we moved, I was expected to get rid of a considerable quantity of toys. It wasn't too bad: I'd hold a garage sale and be extremely popular for the day. After all, who else is going to sell you 250 marbles for fifty cents? But I do remember having the distinct impression that everyone thought my treasures were expendable."

Which brings us to two cardinal rules for cleaning out: (1) Don't throw away any child's possession without consulting your child. He may decide to give it away or to sell it in a yard sale, but let the decision be his. The space you may save in the packing just isn't worth the upset. (2) Don't leave anything behind—a swing set that's impossible to move, a piano that can't fit through the door—without first explaining to your child *before* the move. One ten-year-old boy said he was angry with his mother for weeks because she had left his train set behind without telling him. She explained that the big table it had been glued to was impossible to get out of the cellar. That may have been true enough, but it was small consolation to a boy who suddenly found he was without his train set. So your child will be prepared for the loss explain the situation before the move. Then he may want to take

pictures of the things he loves that won't be coming with him and paste them in *Goodbye, House.*

Encourage your child to pack his own toys and belongings. Be sure to label the carton so it can be found easily when you arrive.

• **Make plans with your child for moving day.** To have the kids around or not to have them around on moving day is the question. The move might be a lot easier if they were at a friend's or relative's house. But some children might feel neglected. So talk with each child to see how he or she feels and if and how you can accommodate these feelings.

If your children will be there on moving day, sit down beforehand and make a list of simple chores they'll be responsible for. The children will feel that they're needed and you'll feel relieved that they won't be getting in the way.

• **Consider the children's interests when packing the van.** It may be worth considering whether you'd like the movers to put your children's furniture and belongings in the van last so they can be the first to be taken out on arrival. Getting the kids' rooms set up first not only reassures them that they have a "home" in their new house or apartment, but—on the practical side—gives them a place to stay out of the way. They can be involved in arranging their rooms while you oversee the rest of the unpacking.

• **Celebrate your arrival.** Children have a real sense of ceremony. Perhaps you can arrange to have a special toast when you first arrive at your new home: champagne for the adults, and milk and cookies for the children.

• **Make the first night in your new home comfortable for your children.** One ten-year-old child couldn't fall asleep in the New York City apartment he moved to because, as he pointed out to his father, his bedroom was closest to the front door, so if any robbers broke in they would get to him first. Children may need extra reassurance until they feel comfortable in their new home. We've suggested to your child that he might like a flashlight in his room the first night.

• **Let your child help decorate her room.** Children love to decorate their own rooms. If you can arrange to give your child a fair amount of authority in this process, it will help her gain a sense of mastery over her new environment. For instance, if the rooms are to be painted, allowing your child to help choose the color of her room might make her happy. You might want to promise her one new thing for her room, such as a new bedspread or a big bulletin board.

• **Help your child make new friends.** The biggest fear children expressed to us is that the new kids wouldn't like them. Nobody would even want to talk to them. Nobody their age would live in their neighborhood. As one seven-year-old girl put it: "What if I have to walk someplace or go near a cemetery and I don't have a friend?"

Each child has his own pace when making new friends and becoming familiar with the neighborhood. Some kids are eager to start. Others need more time. Whatever the pace of your child, respect it and don't push too hard. You can help best by being available to facilitate the process. On that score, here are some suggestions from children:

1. Many children say it's awkward to walk over by themselves and knock on a neighbor's door to see if there are any kids to play with. If that's how your child feels, you can help by going with her and introducing yourself to your new neighbors while she meets the children in the house.

2. You might want to remind your child that very often the excitement of the moving van will bring neighborhood kids over to see what's going on. If possible, have lemonade and cookies on hand.

3. Children report that one of the best ways to get to know the neighborhood is to bicycle or take a walk with a neighborhood child. The new neighborhood friend can point out where other children live and play. Some children say it's helpful if a neighborhood friend draws a map for them.

4. Some kids may need encouragement at first to invite new friends over. By all means make your children feel that, even if the condition of the house is less than perfect, they're welcome to bring friends home.

5. As was true before the move, children need your special attention after the move, too. More story time before bed, walks and drives together to explore the area—all will help reassure your child that, no matter what, he's still got you.

6. The more social networks you set up, the better for your child. If you join a church or synagogue, the children can start going to Sunday school and making friends there. Joining the local Y can bring the entire family into contact with new people. Joining the parents' organization at your children's school will help them feel you're part of their community. By meeting parents of children the same age as yours, you will begin to develop a network of people to ask about clubs, scouting programs, Little League, and other activities that you think your children might be interested in.

• **Help your child prepare for the first day of school.** Whether your child arrives during the school year or begins school with the rest of the children, the first day of school can be frightening. A number of projects in *Goodbye, House* are designed to help your child prepare for it and feel comfortable when she walks into her new school. In addition, there are a number of things you can do in advance to help make the first day of school as problem-free as possible.

1. Write ahead to the school principal to get answers to questions that both you and your child might have about the new school: How large is the school? What is the curriculum? Will any foreign languages be taught? Are any special supplies required (gym uniform, books)? It can be traumatic, for instance, for a third grader to go into his new class to find that all the kids already know script and he doesn't. The more he knows about the class's speed relative to his own, the better.

2. You may also need to know what special documents are necessary for enrollment: for example, your child's birth certificate and doctor's records. You can put these papers into an envelope to have them handy when you arrive at your new home.

3. Now is also the time to arrange for your children's school records to be forwarded to their new schools.

4. In *Goodbye, House* we suggest to your child that she might want to get a pen pal from the new school before she arrives. You could help by calling or writing the school to ask for the name and address of a student who might be willing—and most probably delighted—to take on the responsibility. Not only will your child get some sense of the new school from her pen pal, she will have a built-in friend when she arrives.

5. If possible, you might want to arrange to go with your child to meet his teacher before the first day of school. Then he can see the classroom and get a sense of the layout of the school, and the teacher can show him some of the books he will be using and what he will be learning. Also, by finding out something about your child in advance, the teacher will be better able to introduce him to the class. The more the teacher can tell the class about your child, the more questions the other kids can ask him about himself.

6. Depending on your child's age and needs, you may want to accompany her on the trip to school for the first few days. Or an older brother or sister or a child in the neighborhood could be the one to take her.

7. Check your child's progress in school during the first few months. If there are any problems, talk with the teacher. You might decide to arrange for special help so he can catch up in subjects in which he may be behind.

Eventually your child will make friends and settle in to her new home and school. By then "where we used to live" will be a warm memory to be recalled with pleasure. Once the adjustment is made and *Goodbye, House* is completed, make sure that the book is kept safely so that it can be treasured along with other childhood mementos long after your child is making her own moves in the world.